IN ACCELERATED

SILENCE

IN ACCELERATED

SILENCE

poems by

BROOKE MATSON

Jake Adam York Prize ✳ Selected by Mark Doty

MILKWEED EDITIONS

Published 2020 by Milkweed Editions
Printed in Canada
Cover design by Mary Austin Speaker
Cover artwork: Eagle Nebula by Gorän Nilsson via Creative Commons
Attribution-ShareAlike 4.0 International License
20 21 22 23 24 5 4 3 2 1
First Edition

Milkweed Editions, an independent nonprofit publisher, gratefully acknowledges
sustaining support from the Alan B. Slifka Foundation and its president, Riva Ariella
Ritvo-Slifka; the Ballard Spahr Foundation; *Copper Nickel*; the Jerome Foundation;
the McKnight Foundation; the National Endowment for the Arts; the National
Poetry Series; the Target Foundation; and other generous contributions from
foundations, corporations, and individuals. Also, this activity is made possible by
the voters of Minnesota through a Minnesota State Arts Board Operating Support
grant, thanks to a legislative appropriation from the arts and cultural heritage fund.
For a full listing of Milkweed Editions supporters, please visit milkweed.org.

Library of Congress Cataloging-in-Publication Data

    Names: Matson, Brooke, author.
    Title: In accelerated silence : poems / Brooke Matson.
    Description: First edition. | Minneapolis, Minnesota : Milkweed
    Editions,
      2020. | Identifiers: LCCN 2019022503 (print) | LCCN 2019022504
    (ebook) | ISBN
      9781571315151 (trade paperback ; acid-free paper) | ISBN
    9781571317353
      (ebook)
    Classification: LCC PS3613.A8386 A6 2020 (print) | LCC PS3613.
    A8386
      (ebook) | DDC 811/.6--dc23
    LC record available at https://lccn.loc.gov/2019022503
    LC ebook record available at https://lccn.loc.gov/2019022504

for Ryan

There will be music despite everything.
—JACK GILBERT,
"A BRIEF FOR THE DEFENSE"

CONTENTS

IN ACCELERATED

SILENCE

I

ODE TO DARK MATTER

I speed through the moonless
night—porch lights thinning

into silhouettes of trees.
Emptiness isn't empty,

the radio scientist insists. Relieved
you're here to hold the aching

stars apart, a muted backdrop to the howl
of headlights streaking by, I bend

the pedal to the floor.
His voice describes a mine

deep under the earth
where professors hunt the flutter

of your wings
in accelerated silence—

wait for you to slip, to exhale
into their sensitive machine, eager

to assemble your breath
in data streams. They think

you're already theirs:
a variable to ensnare in a net sum,

the way children trust
answers to soothe.

Dear wild unknown: tow the borders
of this universe far beyond

our grasp. Whatever we see, we break—
count and dismember

all we touch:
The earth. The atom. Anatomy. Eve.

Be the animal that escapes
our love without a wound.

ELEGY IN THE FORM OF A POMEGRANATE

Eve was like that: eating a pomegranate
like smashing a chest of rubies.
She split the whole

vermilion world in a violent need to know.
My finger circles the crown, traces its tight circumference,
red and round. I pluck it from the mound

the grocer arranged and hear the question
I asked you that night, when we were just beginning
to trust each other: *If I were a fruit, what would I be?*

The Latin for fruit is *pōmum*
and some reading that Bible believed Eve
ate an apple. I hold your answer

in my hand: *You are striking. Tough to crack.*
Worth every effort, you said. There's an art
to eating a pomegranate. Cut away the crown

until you see the chambers inside—six bedrooms
shining with scarlet chandeliers. In a bowl of water
use your thumbs to tear the walls apart.

I wonder if you ever ate a pomegranate
this way when alive, and if you wanted—
the way Eve wanted—to be understood, to understand,

to be freed from your flesh like a hundred supple seeds.
But this is a supermarket, not a bedroom,
and my cart is empty

and I am wavering on the scuffed linoleum
of the produce aisle, rubbing the skin of a pomegranate
as if it were your hand.

THE DAY BEFORE

the doctor called we whispered
over a white-clothed table
in my favorite restaurant, sipping ruby

bulbs of Malbec. You weren't hungry
(a symptom, we later learned) but insisted
I order the portobello.

Like magnets, our knees
locked beneath the table, a phenomenon
you loved to point out. Waiters hummed

around candles like sable bees
and evening honeyed the sills.
We're gonna do everything right, you said,

setting down your glass and grinning—
meaning July, Seattle, meaning
two children and long retirement.

I couldn't help it. I reached
across the tablecloth to touch the lines
at the corner of your eye.

It took you by surprise, my thumb
brushing your skin as if painting
the edge of you.

RED GIANT

Light ground to silver powder, suspended in a syringe
the nurse slid into your vein. *I tasted metal*

you mused after, as if it were an experiment
not a hunt for cells intent

on your death, not an ore that could solder
your body to life. We didn't know

technetium has a half-life
of four million years. It burns in the bellies

of red giants—stars smoldering
at the end of their lives—a highlight

before the collapse into gravity. *I feel sick*
you said. We agreed it must be

that terrible metal. *I'll sleep it off*
you said. We didn't know

the isotope that laced your veins
was stripped from fuel rods,

old nuclear reactors—
a chemical back-burn to fight the fire

igniting your scan, igniting your left
brain like the night sky.

It must still be there in the soil:
rust from the ribs of the stars

dividing in the rind of your skull, scissoring
one life into many.

SUPERMASSIVE STAR

Let there be—

you said, and assembled me from fusion / fire / a timer
set in motion

For every reaction   an equal
opposite contraction

Don't pretend you're not
a part of this
You called me here
                              to burn

You called and I came
willingly
                    lit
like a birthday wish

Your auric
          little miracle
Your magic machine

I clapped my hands   ignited
every color until the trick

backfired   /
                              until
one dense atom
spun in my core   a thin

                    spider

          of iron

          and so began the collapse /
          compacting mass / the glorious
punch
          of gravity

               Your word was my death
                                   sutured within me

MAYBE

Who is the You *in your poems,* he asks, because it is capitalized.
Do I have to know? I haven't been to Mass since Death
(capital *d*) entered the narrative and sent my heart palpitating
with rage at nothing in particular, because who can be blamed
for unexplained cancer? *You need to figure it out,* he says, as in
dissect the pronoun. In middle school, my classmate refused
to dissect a grasshopper, the exoskeleton limp on its aluminum
tray. She came to class the next day with a grasshopper formed
from clay, each appendage painted in immaculate rainbow
colors. It glowed on the teacher's desk, hovered above the
lesson plan on its stand, a vibrant idol outsizing all the dead
ones put together. I suppose that was her point. Now my point.
Am I avoiding the question? Our universe may be one of many
in the Multiverse (capital *m*)—*may be* as in *maybe,* as in
somewhere on the spectrum between *yes* and *no,* one of several
enigmatic answers the Magic 8 Ball we had as kids offered
from its dark indigo fluid, a tiny triangular phrase bumping
the window in its belly. One day ours stopped answering—
something about the buoyancy, or maybe one of us just
shook it too hard.

NEUROSURGERY

I've imagined it many times and still it jars
like a fist to the jaw. *There will be music
despite everything*, you quoted, and yes, my pulse
quickens, even now, at Zoë Keating's electric
cello, enough to need tissues.
I imagine it so often, it's as if I saw

the surgeon, swathed like a priest, drive the saw
into your skull. Like popping the seal of a mason jar,
he unhinges blood and bone, exposes the grey tissue
of his trade. The nurse presses *play* on our music
as instructed (cue the cello); nerves bathe in electric
oceans; the pulse

of cello strings drop like plumb lines through the pulsing
Z of the heart monitor. I believe you hear it. But that saw
haunts me—some real Frankenstein shit. *Where's the electric
bolt of lightning*, you'd joke, but I can't laugh. The jarring
raze of its serrations cleaves the music,
cleaves my tissue-

thin bravery. I have learned time is a flexible tissue
and the muscled pulse
of your neurons strums its own shining music:
our first kiss on a darkened street; the seesawing
oars of kayaks on the bay; whiskey sipped from jam jars
on the Fourth of July; fireworks glowing electric

as you rise between thighs, electrified—
years of time folded tightly in a cortex maze of tissue
where somewhere, my body wanders through synapses that jar
and flicker like Vegas highways, pulsations
of neon in contiguous, cursive constellations. Tell me sawing
stars from the sky is impossible, that music

can't be severed from melody, the cellist from the musical
oscillations of her instrument, the wild electron
from the nucleus it loves. Say there is not a saw
for every bond. Say that our minds are not lanterns of tissue
paper, easily torn. Your pulse
holds you together a while—a fragile jar

of stars humming their music in the dark tissue
of space, an electric dance of neurons. Like hope, they pulse.
O trade me a saw for a spoon, that I may scrape the sides of
    that jar.

EVE SPLITS THE APPLE

We were given so much—the entire field
unbroken by boundary. The colors—
you should have seen them: black sheen
of the beetle, indigo silk of the river rippling under
the tiger's flat tongue. What I'm trying to say

is I knew nothing of law
even as I spotted its blushing throb
fastened high, like the sun to the sky.
Or maybe that I loved its red
as I loved the pulse inside

his chest, my ear pressed to his flesh on nights
we held each other on banana leaves, his body
moving over me, moving against the rheumy
field of stars. I loved its orb, its warmth,
and its waxy shine—even as I tore it from the limb

that bore it, split the sphere
on a stone, half its sugared meat
for each of us. I didn't know you can break
against laws. He smiled when he saw
what I'd brought, brushed my hair behind

my shoulder as he took my gift.
Even before he bit, I foresaw his jaw
fall from his white skull; the doe
slit open by the puma, her lustrous muscles
flayed against the grass;

saw the leaves departing,
scarlet, from maple trees—then
an ashen fence of rain, a flood. Even before
he swallowed. Before the sword of light
severed what lay behind.

BROADEN THE SUBJECT

In kindergarten the teacher
asked, *What kind of things are
red?* and arms rocketed
toward the ceiling with
apples firetrucks roses.
I raised my hand and said,
*Anything can be red, like a
sweater or a crayon,* and Mrs.
Curley's face fell and she
· said, *No, things that are
always red.* But my favorite
apple is yellow, I thought,
the same frustration as
when my friend tells me to
broaden my focus, to think
about moving on to another
metaphor, and maybe I *am*
a bull anchored to what
hurts, charging sentences at
what I cannot understand:
a cluster of small hands
firing into the air like
flags, symbols of how
the world ought to be.
I ought to let it go—maybe.
I return to red red red
because I cannot let it go
or turn my head the way
most people focus on the
positive—*flower* not *blood,*·
pomegranate not *wound.*
Maybe I am the narrow hot

line at the edge of the
visible spectrum, inching
toward invisible, bordering
on irrelevant. Understand:
anything can be red,
usually when someone or
something splits open.

II

LAW OF THE CONSERVATION OF MASS

i. Big Bang

Maybe there was a word—
a short, single syllable that fell
like a long-traveled drop

of rain and shuddered
a seed of light
into a flock of starlings,

wildfires of wings.
How long till matter
clotted like drops of mercury

into planets and moons and stars,
into a pulse
and a brain that believed?

ii. Trinity Test Site

The bright plume
that blossomed from the ground was a voice

crying, *Stop.*

When I touch your photograph
on the refrigerator, the spiral of my fingerprint
marks your cheek

like a small halo of cloud.
Life doesn't wait, I hear you say.

Outside, the starlings sing
the afternoon to grey while lilacs
abandon their fragrance.

iii. Operating Room

The thin knife that severed your tumor—
severed you

from your body—
it cleaves me still.

Those dead scientists asked a question that killed
and we are still

dying slowly from the answer.
Microscopic cells swell like buds

of peony—swell and split
like that first flower of fire.

iv. Hiroshima

Think of a lit match—
how its head vanishes.

v. Fallout

All light was once matter
and all matter shall become light.

Evening draws me back
into this bedroom, as it did on days we woke

together, when your fingers found the sheet
and pulled it the extra inch to cover

my bare shoulder. The starlings sing
at morning and evening,

the same doorway—sing
though the hollow your hips

carved on the bed has no mass
to hold its shape. I want to be folded whole

into the light that fills your place.

OUR LADY OF GUADALUPE

In the hammock of his robes, she piles roses
like a bounty of heads—

swollen apologies
from the blue cistern of sky.

Why burden a boy with these soft bodies,
washed, like the dead, with rain?

Go, she said, *and show no one.* I used to keep her
on my kitchen mantel, the spangled

bloom of her body papered around the tall
glass candle, the light-filled mandorla splintering

behind her. As a teen, I had a friend who loved
his faith so much he tattooed her down

the length of his spine, nape
to hip. I watched drops of water star

the corona of her veil as he slid
from the lake at summer camp and told myself

all love was a devotion. Now roses rot
on the side of my house, withered husks

of sparrows I slap
from stems. When I learned remission

was out of reach, I hurled
the candle across the room. A vessel

was all I wanted—beatitude of wax,
axiom of *I understand, I intercede,* a reprieve

whispered in the dark, where our bodies weigh
as much as rose-scent. Once I massacred

a rosebush, not knowing to cut
above the bud eye,

how each limb feeds
the next like a vein, how the arms

can dry up like rivers, dammed. I slammed
that heavy candle in the trash. It sank

like a full bottle of wine.
Anticlimactic. Cliché. Not enough, I tore

her icon from the wall—the one I lacquered
onto cedar that summer

as a teen. My initials
at the bottom—who was she?

METAPHORS OF MASS DESTRUCTION

1. Cancer:

the typist's fingers miss a key
on the invite

taking care to bend the brads
she hand-delivers
the manila

upon receipt the President
launches a missile

2. Fission:

her grandmother's necklace snaps
at the party
            freshwater pearls
            riot

    ricochet

        roll

under the sink
down heat shafts

look   you'll never find them all
besides   the string is broken

3. Grief:

a fingertip traces the rim
of an empty wineglass
until it

    howls

PSALM OF THE ISRAELI GRENADE

Six hundred and thirteen seeds of a pomegranate
are six hundred and thirteen commandments
of scripture singing lead rivets

in the ribs of the enemy. I am the mitzvah arcing
through their open windows hung with thyme.
Into their lemon orchards, chartreuse heads

broken like dandelions
in a hurricane. Centuries shorn to ash
in nanoseconds—a psalm of cinders

over scored land. Each death
sends a chorus of detonations ringing
like rain on the Red Sea. The waves

pass through one another
as ghosts walk
through walls. I want to sing, Father.

Pull the ring of the pin and release me—
a red dove erupting from the cliffside, russet earth
blown heavenward on a burnt

offering of belief. Isn't that
Your unspoken commandment? A slaughtered ram
at Rosh Hashanah: *may we be head not tail.*

Not the wailing. Not the carcass
carried through the streets.
But the dark sun

sailing through a kitchen window. The crack
of light lifting feet. Brow split
like a pomegranate within a kerchief.

NEWTON'S APPLE

Came to him casually, a wild syllable
    of color, a ripe proposition.

Bruised on the grass, a casual reminder
    of our entrance on the earth.

Anchored to field, a weight
    that tipped the scale,

Eclipsed the sun, the pocket of its blushing
    body burnished.

Cleaved his angular thoughts like a joke.

Weighed in the cup of his hand, a mass
    of lead, of red, of laughter.

Dropped again to be sure.

Bruised again / again / again /

PRISM

i. Dissection

Morning shatters a water glass, casts
rainbows on formica.

I am not fooled. Don't try to convince me
any of these are promises. I've lost

too much—his curves
immersed in earth while flowers and berries and birds
make use. What could You possibly

offer me now?
                    An empty glass.

A man pared
into colors. His laughter peeled
away like the skin of an apple.

ii. Black

Priests wear black to tell their flock, *I am already dead
and therefore cannot die.*

We should all wear black—not only
for mourning. Ashes every day
as protest.

Obsidian that shoulders the quiet
story of fire.

Black like outer space—
the balance of probability between her hips.

I say *her* because like Eve she does not
obey the law.

She eats whatever she likes.

iii. Death

The prism we pass through.

The nameless blade
that strips us to wavelengths.

Narrow bridge we cross
into the body of another.

iv. White

The science teacher crossed three spotlights on the wall:
green, blue, and red.

My hypothesis was grey. Others
said purple, surely. Or brown.

He darkened the room, slid
each over the other: a triangle of pristine white

light
where they collected.

Explain this, he said.

                    Not one of us could.

v. Wake

Can light break
or does it, like water, extend

into ocean, conform
to its container, swallow all assaults, never shatter

no matter how many stones
you throw?

vi. Electromagnetic field

I didn't intend to end up here.

I didn't mean to go beyond
black and white, our beginning

and his ending, beyond the fence of the visible
spectrum. I find myself wandering, like Hertz and Ritter,

into sound and temperature—other
means of communication.

vii. Others

                   slide through us:

ossified X-rays drift like smoke, the husks
of broken bones. Infrared waves

slither over summer streets. Ultraviolets
singe skin while gammas punch holes
in every cell they find.

They, too, believe in their solitude.

They, too, try to notch
a word into the world.

viii. Waves

It was never my intention to return to the beginning.
Never

to return to this field—
to the bright spring day that followed
his departure. It was here—

right here I trod a path through the tall grass.
It rippled like an ocean

in every direction—hemmed together
where my body passed through.

ELEGY IN THE FORM OF AN OCTOPUS

I gasp when her body ripples from rust
to silver. Her tentacles fumble the mussel
at the edge of the tank. I've been

that desperate lately, willing to break
delicate things for hunger's sake, like the ivory
dishes that recall the years

before we met. How satisfying to split
the discs against patio concrete, to abandon
carloads of furnishings at Goodwill

and imagine my grief tucked in the bags.
Strong emotions cause her to change color
the biologist explains as she transfigures

into a knot of red caught on a twig,
a deflated balloon in a breeze. An octopus
is smarter than a house cat. Her eye

flicks in my direction, every cell hinged
on listening. No exoskeleton means vulnerability.
I press a hand to the glass and her ruddy skin

peppers with white the way my neck
felt like rain each time you grazed it. She heaves
her body over her quarry like a paper lantern

set over a flame. If I could have plucked you
like a mussel from your shell
I would have swallowed you whole.

III

EVE'S APPLE

Became soft, browned flesh—eucharist
    dissolved on a tongue where it

Dropped

Bruised among the leaves.

Gnawed by badgers.

Drunk by moths.

Succumbed to hordes of ants ascending in the night.

Filed to a spire of seeds, the rind bending
    toward the field.

Illuminated under the crescent moon,
    a slender skull
    with five narrow eyes.

Tempted away from shape—

Leaned toward sugar, toward myth.

Imprinted on the field, an indented
    cup of scent—the urgent press
    of her question.

LAW OF INERTIA

A pair of sandals suspended
near the front door, the
same that walked beside
him on the shore, their gold
straps worn to grey. Call
them artifacts of a woman
who died. I've left my body
far behind since the funeral.
Their haphazard stance
spells tragedy, waiting for
hands to arrive that might
cradle them like relics—
reverent and ridiculous as
this woman here, unable to
bury the year-old bag of rice
in the garbage pail because
his thick fingers once
pressed the seal, or to sell
the · couch where our
shoulders and thighs
etched the polyester-linen
blend. How comfortable we
both declared the cushions
and how holy it seems now
—the padded springs still
insist on his shape.

IMPOSSIBLE THINGS

It is impossible to spontaneously create quark from vacuum, but yet it happens all the time. —DR. MACIEJ LEWICKI

There is an 83.2% probability

> webs of mycelium have eaten
> your nerve endings
> and detritus curls like leaves
>
> in the nest of your aorta. You lie
> beside your father, twenty years
> and two feet of earth
>
> between. Mary comes every Sunday
> to lay flowers and say three words for me.

There is an 11.4% probability

> you sit beside your father
> outside the dimension of time. He taps
> a pipe on his bottom teeth,
>
> takes a pull. Galaxies emerge
> from his exhale. Black holes hover
> about his head, the bold scent
>
> of tobacco. *What is the nature of darkness?*
> *Am I unborn?* The words form
> but cannot escape before

he opens a book. Thin sheets of scripture
fan in frothy waves of the sea, whales
cascading between his fingers. He grins

and you fall in, your sea-grey
eyes open wide.

There is a 3.6% probability

> your body escaped by train, a torn
> one-way ticket in your breast pocket.
> The carriage rocks

> back and forth, bullets over the gold-
> green tapestry of countryside at the speed
> of light. Your godmother

> uses the tip of her finger to mark
> your brow with vermilion
> as if something entered there. As if

> something escaped. You turn
> to steam as the train leans
> on a curve, leans

> into sweetgrass, jasmine,
> colors that vanish as you think their names.

There is a 1.79% probability

> your blood has given birth to begonias
> everywhere it fell: in the woods where you scraped
> your knee as a boy, behind the football field

where your mouth tasted his knuckles,
along the dock where ropes cut lines
in your palms. Red lips

chew their way through loam.
They open. They have things to say.

There is a 0.01% probability

you are a great blue whale in the Pacific
culling a seam of morning krill.
You swallow a barrelful, pulse

your larynx like a drum,
surge skyward.
Near the coast of Washington,

a woman wakes, cold
in a strange bed, thinking
she heard your voice.

ELECTRON CLOUD

You tell me of an invisible planetary system in which electrons
gravitate around a nucleus. You explain this world to me with an
image. I realize then that you have been reduced to poetry.
                                        —ALBERT CAMUS

You could be anywhere—

after all, the hummingbird's wings
flutter so fast only
                        a flute of emerald

hovers among the trumpet vines
Even the waspish leaves
hum
            like tuning forks

All matter orbits what it adores

                *

Think of the blades of a fan—
how they cease
to be blades

and where they escaped

a ring

        *

Your palm presses
between my breasts as I unbend
from sleep   my blood

begs like ravens
but the bedroom I wake to is empty—

no—
filled with light but the point is

you were here   you
could be anywhere

                    *

Some days I pause by the rotary phone
to spin the letters of your name

winding back time
in the hum and clack

of the wheel—reeling you in

          letter
                    by letter
Never mind

that it's not plugged in
I swear to god some days

          I hear a crackling on the other end

like the time you called from the hospital
still unable to speak

I stood barefoot on the linoleum
listening to you breathe

even then
                    I believed

CENTRIFUGAL FORCE

I wait for the fabric
    to break—
for a hole to yawn
    through the skin—
but paper-thin it spins
    and spins   the chef's
hardened hands
    have tossed this dough
for years   the disc
    flutters above
and around him
    a Dalí clock falling
and rising with every brush
    of his knuckles   let no one tell you
grief is a stone
    it is supple   a plane
beyond moan
    stretched past the edge
of the known—

ORIONID METEOR

What you call a shower,
I call fire. I've come
this close—

ice and dust and desire
serrated against your cornea.

Friction is a terrible thing.

Trying to touch your face is like singing
as you're burned at the stake—
a colorful prayer
of conversion—

a flaying

just to glimpse your back.
Your catatonic blue. God-iris

almost in focus. A cold ocean to slake
my incinerating question.

ELEGY IN THE FORM OF
ENDANGERED SPECIES

We believe in the seen and unseen—
in blue whales beneath the Strait of Juan de Fuca

gliding like cellos
through silver arteries of salmon

I believed the motel owner who told
of whitecapped waves and a cliff

whales lifting their weight
from water
and before that   a forest

with strange forms of animal
shades of wing
skins I'd never seen

       I've come looking for proof

of what I cannot touch   your body
for instance

        I felt it next to me
last night in that strange bed   rolled
onto your shoulder
           wishful
and necessary thinking

But the rainforest I tread this morning
is thick with silence—
sunlight muted by spruce

Evidence found thus far:

                stained glass of gossamer
                            sans spider

            hovel of a rubber boa   but not the slash
                        of its sentence

                                    At last
after the slick boards of a bridge
I stand on the wingtip

of the map   scanning the bright
horizon

Spouts rise like smoke
but not the dull blade
            of the body—what I crave
                                        Whales

I declare to the man
who has climbed with his wife behind me

            Where?
                        he demands   *There* I say and point
but already it's mist

THERE IS A ROOM IN THE FOUR DIMENSIONS OF THE SPACE-TIME CONTINUUM

where candlelight warms our winter bed
and moon-white hips trace ellipses

around the sun of your skin.
There is a kitchen embedded
in the fibers of time

where your chest trembles
under my hands as a soup pot rattles
on the stove. In the dark

theatre of space, amateur actors
unravel Shakespeare, and as the lights
go down I lean

into your lips as shadows lean
into walls. An entryway exists
where your index finger traces

the boundary of my jaw as I slide
into sleep, as if to unlatch
its gate and enter. Enter

an entire hall—longer than a light-year—
where our knees touch
under tables

and the clinking of glasses glitters
like newly born stars. The corner booth
of our first shared smile

waits heavy with wine, bold as a planet
charting its arc. The entire house
is ours—it is always ours.

IV

ELEGY IN THE FORM OF PORCELAIN

winter is a prism in reverse / colors

reassembling into white

snow that illumines

the morning / kisses the dark

needles of pine / the season

before his death / it crusted the patio

like porcelain from plates I split

against it

months later in my rage / all the delicate

flowers arranged in jagged blue

and alabaster triangles / a kaleidoscope

of edges / fine powder

lost between them / the drifting debris

of dead stars / what I mean is

I loved the brushstrokes

at the corners of his eyes / little hairline

fissures / I mean

we are more than our breaks / what cannot

be reconstructed from the bang

or the plate before / spinning like a galaxy

across the porch

SONNET IN THE HIGGS FIELD

I force my heft against an unseen fence

every morning   just to climb out of bed

Each limb lead-heavy as if fighting tar

a drag that scientists call *mass* and I

call *massive depression*   A relentless

resistance as when skiing on the lake

the raft flipped and I did not release the

rope but clutched it harder   felt my bones moan

against the force of water   a translucent

field of green where trout parted like rays

of light against my ribs and snagged the cold

space of silence   When at last I let go

I became weightless   afraid   a buoyant

breathless particle nameless on the waves

ODE TO A FRACTURED CONCH

You could have been home
to a hermit crab
when I spied you in the sand
imagining you whole—
inspiration for a poem
about fractals
      I dreamt the night before
of Mandelbrot's prime numbers
repeated
in a man's curls
each of which represented a proportion
of the universe
telescoping upon
its verb
a golden chorus played over
and over
      You breathe
water in my hand
throat
cracked through
salt and empty rooms
      No evidence of the voice
I was taught to listen to as a child
      Can you hear it
my sister insisted
pressing the cool
lip to my ear until I was sure

I could
      I believed it was that easy
to commune with the dead
our songs
wound within us like a spool
of string from which
one could reconstruct
the chorus of our origin
      But the silence segmented
in the stairwell
sentence of your body
is somehow
expected
as when walking among the infinite
arms of ferns
later this afternoon
I will find a dead house finch
its breast peeled
back like a husk of corn

ELEGY IN THE FORM OF STEAM

The teakettle quiets before it whistles
and in that breath I recall
the way your hands did simple tasks

with great intention: crushing garlic
with the thick ball of your palm,
stirring soup like it could be injured.

Making the bed, you took your time
smoothing the crease of the top sheet
like soil over newly planted seeds.

The weight of your hand at rest
comforted the silver handle
as you waited for a shrill scream

to cloud the air, a confirmation
of what was real. I grasp
its slender shoulder, lift its body

from the burner. My contents
falter as its cry
falls cold.

METAMORPHOSIS

i. Cocoon

Your mother smoothed the paper
of your face when she believed you were asleep,

wandered into hospital corners to tuck
her tears between glossy magazines.

And now spring licks this side of the earth
and all the rooted, leaf-winged creatures

remember their past lives in the sun.
Green beaks thrust through loam, yawn

for light and dew. You begged me
not to watch your skeleton emerge

from your skin, having witnessed
your father's metamorphosis

at only seventeen. But see
how the soil writhes:

a menagerie of vibrant plumes, supple stalks
splitting into peonies.

See how the cells of your brain become
clouds of cottonwood seed

adrift in the humid heat.

ii. Luna

More animal than insect. More mouse
than moth.

Abdomen long as a robin. Wings
ragged as tissue paper.

It crawled through the cedar shards
of the flowerbed under the amber porch light.

A few steps, double-back,
and it was gone.

I was twelve and breasts
budded under my shirt.

I lay awake.
Under the blinds

the sky beat with the color of sinew,
the glistening shade of lip

and tongue, the shiny intestines of the starling
our cat left coiled

on the doorstep. The moon slid
higher in the frame. I knew

there were spaces inside us
that ache toward light.

iii. Lacuna

When people ask, *How are you?*
my mouth fills with flannel.

How are you doing?
they ask, and I touch the fragile arm

of the sugar bowl
or rather, the hollow

inside its porcelain elbow
where your finger nested

in half-formed thought.
The teakettle howls silver

like a wounded fox
and sometimes I let it howl

until the cat hides under the armchair
because that's when your hand

would relieve it. I wash the rubbered skin
of a bell pepper, cut away the spire

of seeds that scatter
in the sink, hollow its reddened ribs

to a carcass
warm enough to crawl inside.

V

HOW TO EAT A POMEGRANATE
After Sarah Koenig

Don't think about the consequences.
Let the primal need to know
fill you with salt. You will carry its tight
belly in the pocket of your coat
for three days, embrace the weight

of the question—a ripe confession,
a reticent guest. I know
you'd rather have a simple task—
fruit with a softened peel, puckered cheek
that yields to a dull edge.

But that's not why you're here.
If this is sacrifice, don't dilute
the amplitude of the act.
One muscled blow
will sling your skin with magenta.

When you begin, an absence
will open at the back of your throat
the way an astronaut entering space feels the floor
fall away. Don't hesitate.
Use your hands

to scrape the seeds like answers
to your tongue. You will lap
jelly from your palms, bend your fingernails
backward with asking. Do not be ashamed
of the bold carpet stain—

red, relentless proof.

ELEGY IN THE FORM OF A BUTTERFLY BUSH

I pared the boughs back every few months
to keep the twigs from scraping shingles

on the southern side of the shed. Hummingbirds
would make their spry appearances, flit

through sprigs of lilac, vanish
when the shade shifted.

The day they removed the second tumor
from his brain, I stumbled into the garden.

There it stood, silver-limbed and hardy
in the noonday glare. I borrowed an axe.

Hacked it down to an ashen foot. Snapped
the long limbs into sticks.

Months after the funeral, now strong enough
to venture out of doors, thin

and swathed in a robe, what a shock
to see it full and flourishing and larger than before—

hummingbirds dashing between branches
like watercolor brushes.

LITHIUM

Fine like talc. The dust of doves. Faith
you can rub between fingers.
I know you want to believe in objectivity

but let me tell you: your perception
of this moment floats like a darkroom photograph
in a wash of chemistry. Clarity

is what you desire. The fine details. The iris
of his eye daring into focus. I can give you clarity.
I was the red in first fires—a restless, reactive alkali.

When Robert Lowell slept on poets' lawns
and believed he could halt
traffic with his arms, I recognized the deficiency

in his rabid mania, his melancholia. Listen—
happiness hinges on a fulcrum
of salt and light. David Lovelace said, *I've been accustomed*

to mysteries, holy and otherwise. And don't you want
both water and wine? Divine and human?
Illumination by intermediary

is still illumination. I can be that.
I can be that for you. Lovelace also said,
Some of us take communion or whiskey

or poison. I lay out my wares
and like a scattered flock of rock pigeons
you come tottering to the bread.

SONNET ON A HOOK

Her white-limbed torso flails into your palm
just like the salmon you caught as a boy—

your first fish. The crescent moon of its hip
beat silver on the belly of the boat,

eyes wide and mouth agape. The tightened line
flecked the deck with red, made you sob and beg

to throw it back—to end those brutal oscillations.
Now the perpetual vowel

of her anatomy opens, slaps your palm,
and you are hook and lure and gasping boy

both caught and catching in a woman's hip
so that she bows and arcs supine, a boat

unmoored, her jaw unhinged. Let go the line
of where her body breaks and yours begins.

ODE TO A ROTTING APPLE

And it occurred to me, standing there in that bleak, cavernous space,
that nobody is ever just one thing. . . . If the multiverse was about
choices, and all possible choices were being made, then we might be
all those things and everything in between. —A.W. HILL

Consider yourself a red house
        containing five
        slender black doors   each containing
        a different house
        in a different country

Choose one

Turn the knob like a period that extends
        to comma   that softens the milky
        page of your ribs

Let your bruise be passage
        to your escape / exit / entry

Be trajectory
        gnarled little snake-root
        cracking the rim of a seed   ellipsis
        at the end of the book

Hum at a frequency
        only the dead can hear

Let gravity hold you / unfold you
        into a thousand rooms one for each
        variety of your kind

Recite their names   remember nothing
decides the fate of a body
that speaks the language of *infinite* the lexicon
of *overcome* and this is not their house
their doors

Utter an impossible thing   unfurl green
syllables from a new tongue

Be multiplicity
blossoms freed over the field

Be Honeycrisp / Granny Smith /
Braeburn / Gala / Ambrosia

Construct a new stanza

AMARYLLIS

the amaryllis split this morning into scarlet

tongues   after I made love to him or rather

to his ghost   it's the same now to my body

sometimes I cry but today something shuddered

loose inside me and my brain recited *God*

from God   light from light   true God from true

God and on and on   the whole creed

rushed back to me   I hadn't spoken it in years

and only then in communion with strangers

who filled in gaps where my lips

stumbled   here it was in its entirety

whole beautiful verses   repeating like a song

only weeks ago the amaryllis was a tight fist

on my windowsill   absorbing the thin

light of winter   the ice is so thick

it will never release us   *God from God*

light from light   one plus one plus one

does not equal three but one again   after it wilts

when I cut away the head   another

will rise in its place   and another after that

and another after that

ALCHEMY

since our bodies last kissed   I cry

crossing the ocean between my thighs

it used to be enough

to be a single woman sailing

through her own body   steady

and determined

but now I am rudderless

and longing buoys me toward

the ridged fire of the horizon

into which gulls wheel

and disappear—the crucible

where sailboats melt to gold   arc wide

into the hip of evening

what is it we carve

into each other when the waves

swallow us   when we surface

like survivors   unclear

whether we've woken in paradise

or death   the story

necessitates we continue

that the salt-burned body

keeps breathing

ODE TO THE RETURNED

Give me the wolves that returned to the sea

      eons ago when ocean was old hat and every

            mammal was walking. Give me the sledge

of their legs into surf, the sheet of salt

      drawn across matted fur—a lullaby

            forgotten. The slow erase of an amber iris

for a star of obsidian, the algorithm

      of wind for the gloss of current.

            Claw for fin. Fur for skin. Give me their cold

freedom, the period

      of sun dimming, then blotted

            by depth. Give me the wide comb

of their bellies, throats like sieves,

      the ocean passing through them—growl

            turned to howl, turned to song.

ODE TO THE SUN

cracking the boughs
of my neighbors' pines
with your light—

your first appearance
in what feels like months

let me stand in my bathrobe
one foot in the pantry
the other in the kitchen and lean
to the left

so your fire
finds my irises
I want to be

blinded so when I close
my eyes even then

you are with me—
thumbprint

on the darkness—

NOTES

The poems in this collection first appeared in the following publications:

CALYX: "Elegy in the Form of Steam" (as "Tea Kettle")
Copper Nickel: "Amaryllis"
Crab Creek Review: "Ode to Dark Matter," "Lithium"
Isthmus: "Newton's Apple"
Laurel Review: "Electron Cloud," "Orionid Meteor," "Elegy
   in the Form of Porcelain"
Pacific Northwest Inlander: "Elegy in the Form of a
   Pomegranate" (as "Ode to a Pomegranate")
Permafrost: "Metamorphosis"
Poetry Northwest: "Elegy in the Form of an Octopus" (as "Ode
   to Chromatophores, Ode to an Octopus")
Portland Review: "Impossible Things," "How to Eat
   a Pomegranate"
Potomac Review: "Maybe"
Rock & Sling: "Eve Splits the Apple," "Prism"
Sierra Nevada Review: "Broaden the Subject"
TAYO: "Law of the Conservation of Mass," "Metaphors of
   Mass Destruction"
Willow Springs: "Neurosurgery" (as "Neurosurgery Sonata")

"Electron Cloud," "Eve Splits the Apple," and "Neurosurgery" have been nominated for the 2020 Pushcart Prize by *Laurel Review*, *Rock & Sling*, and *Willow Springs*.

"Psalm of the Israeli Grenade" quotes the Book of Deuteronomy: "May we be head not tail," often used as a blessing for Rosh Hashanah. The final line of the poem is from Song of Solomon 6:7. The line "I want to sing, Father" is borrowed from the Jason Webley song "In This Light."

"Newton's Apple" was inspired by Linda Bierds's poem "Correlation of Physical Forces" from *Roget's Illusion* (New York: Penguin, 2014).

The quote by Dr. Maciej Lewicki in "Impossible Things" was taken from a Quora page titled "What is the probability of quarks spontaneously appearing in a vacuum? Where does the energy come from to create said quarks?"

"Electron Cloud" begins with a quote by Albert Camus from "An Absurd Reasoning," in *The Myth of Sisyphus*, trans. Justin O'Brien (New York: Vintage, 1955).

The quotes by David Lovelace in "Lithium" are from his book *Scattershot: My Bipolar Family* (New York: Dutton, 2008).

"How to Eat a Pomegranate" was inspired by Sarah Koenig's poem "How to Vacuum a Skyscraper" published in *CALYX* 30, no. 1 (Summer/Fall 2017).

ACKNOWLEDGMENTS

My deepest gratitude to the following individuals, who made this collection possible:

Lindsay Hill, for reading this manuscript with the care and precision of a neurosurgeon, and for seeing what I was trying to do before I saw it myself;

Thom Caraway, for his thoughtful, line-by-line feedback that took this manuscript in a better direction at a stage when it badly needed it;

Nance Van Winckel, for encouraging me to aim high;

Lauren Gilmore, Laura Read, Tod Marshall, Dan Peters, Kathryn Smith, Nathaniel Youmans, Devin Devine, and Chris Weppler, for taking the time to read these poems and make them stronger;

Mark Doty, for enjoying my work and choosing this manuscript for the Jake Adam York Prize;

the Artist Trust, which awarded me a Grant for Artist Projects (GAP) with a Centrum residency, in order that I might have the time and solitude needed to complete this manuscript;

Jason Webley, whose live and wildly alive music turned me back to poetry in a critical time of despair (thank you for playing my requests);

and to Neil deGrasse Tyson, for feeding my love of astrophysics and (unknowingly) assisting my poetry with his book, *Astrophysics for People in a Hurry*.

Brittan Hart

Brooke Matson is the author of one previous collection of poems, *The Moons*. Her poems have appeared in *TAYO*, *Potomac Review*, and *Prairie Schooner*, and have been selected for anthologies such as *Towers & Dungeons* and *Railtown Almanac*. She is also a book artist and a recipient of an Artist Trust Grant for Artist Projects and a Centrum residency. She currently resides in Spokane, Washington, where she is the executive director of Spark Central, a nonprofit dedicated to igniting creativity.

The Jake Adam York Prize for a first or second collection of poems was established in 2016 to honor the name and legacy of Jake Adam York (1972–2012). York was the founder of *Copper Nickel*, a nationally distributed literary journal at the University of Colorado Denver. His work as a poet and scholar explored memory and social history, and particularly the Civil Rights Movement.

The judge for the 2018 Jake Adam York Prize was Mark Doty.

Interior design by Mary Austin Speaker
Typeset in Adobe Caslon Pro
by Rodolfo Avelar

Adobe Caslon Pro was created by Carol Twombly
for Adobe Systems in 1990. Her design was inspired by
the family of typefaces cut by the celebrated engraver
William Caslon I, whose family foundry served
England with clean, elegant type from the early
Enlightenment through the turn of the
twentieth century.